COST PER ACTION CASH

MAKE CASH ONLINE WITH CPA MARKETING

I0483204

ANTHONY EKANEM

Contents

Preface

It has never been easier to make money with Cost Per Action (CPA) than it is today. With cost per action, you are paid whenever someone completes an offer, whether it is a sale or lead generation using your referral or affiliate link. There are many Cost Per Action companies available to choose from, each having dozens or even hundreds of offers.

Throughout this guide, you will be introduced to a variety of techniques and strategies that you can use to profit substantially from CPA. These are strategies that have been used by many internet marketers to make money online.

By the time you finish reading this book, you will have a good understanding of what it takes to benefit from Cost Per Action offers and you will also be able to start promoting it immediately.

You may have completed Cost Per Action offers in the past and did not realise that you were giving the person money by downloading software or entering your zip code or email address in a form. Surprisingly, something as simple as providing your email address in a form can result in being paid as much $1.50 in most cases.

When you join a Cost Per Action company, what you are doing is helping that company to promote the advertisers that have registered with that company to promote their product or service. The services of CPA companies are broken down into two categories.

1. The Advertisers

These are companies that pay the Cost Per Action companies to promote their products or services. In most cases, they make a deposit to have their products or services promoted. Once they have made the deposit and the offers go live on the CPA Company's database, they are made available to the advertisers and the publishers.

2. The Publishers

As mentioned earlier, the Advertisers have their company listed with the Cost Per Action Company's database, so it is now available for the Publishers to start promoting. The Publishers are the promoters. You will be the Publisher, as you will be promoting the offers listed within the CPA Company's database by the Advertisers.

That is essentially how CPA networks work. You have the Advertisers and the Publishers. It is also important to note that some Cost Per Action offers have some restrictions, so all the methods that will be mentioned in this book may not apply to every available offer. For instance, some offers may be restricted to email promotion only, while others may be restricted to web and search only.

When an advertiser is setting up their offer, they have the option of choosing the mode of promotion they allow for their offers. Email-only offers are mainly for those who have newsletters or a mailing list to promote their offers. And while the web is for on-site banner placements, the search is mainly for those who advertise through pay-per-click search engines.

You will have the option as a Publisher to go through and select the offers that meet your specifications in terms of mode of promotion. When you join the various CPA networks, you will realise that some offers will be available in more than one CPA network. For example, CPA Network A may have the same offer as CPA Network B.

The difference between the two offers may be the payout that one network is offering. That is why you must join more than one CPA network. Do not put all your eggs in one basket. You will need to join as many CPA networks as possible, so you can review all the offers available in each system and select the one that is paying the most for the offer you would like to promote.

In the next section, you will be introduced to a step-by-step approach to getting accepted into different CPA Networks.

CHAPTER ONE

Getting Accepted into CPA Networks

Before you apply to any CPA Network, you must have a very clear understanding of how you will be promoting the various offers available within the CPA Network. Most CPA networks like to work with veterans within the internet marketing industry, so you must not appear to be a greenhorn when it comes to internet marketing. You will need to understand certain fundamental concepts.

Modes of Promotion

When you review an application form for a CPA network, you will find a list of the different types of promotion that you can choose from as your means of promoting the CPA offers.

You will decide which of the options you will be using to promote your CPA offers. Since it is possible at this stage that you do not know the model you will be using, you should select "Banners", "Text Links", and "PPC" as the options you will be using to promote your CPA offers. Once you are accepted into the network, you can always add more options.

Your job is to ensure you are accepted into the network as quickly as possible and show them that you know what you are doing. The first step before applying for any CPA Network is to have a professional website setup. If you have an old domain name that you have not been using for a long time, then it is time to make use of that domain name. The older the domain name, the better your chances of being accepted into the CPA network. Also, create an email address based on the domain name; that is the email address you will be using to contact the CPA networks, as it is more professional that way.

What you will need to do is to set up a blog. You can create your blog using WordPress that is available for free as your content management system to make things easy to setup. The reason for this is that it is a quick and painless process, and with some of the free themes available online, it can look quite professional without your having to do much work or spend much money setting up your website.

Once you have WordPress set up and installed on your site, you will need a theme to use. You can review these sites below for free themes to use on your blog.

1. www.skinpress.com
2. www.wpskins.org
3. www.freewpthemes.net

Visit the above websites to select a free theme that you can use on your blog. After selecting your theme, and setting up your blog, you will need to pick a niche or topic for your blog, along with having contents. This will be easy since you are not setting up the blog as an eCommerce website that is going to make you money but to show the CPA networks that you have a professional site. This will get approved quickly. The role of this blog is to have a "dummy" site that you can use to get accepted by the CPA network.

As regards the contents of the blog, you can use Private Label Right (PLR) articles. Many sites offer PLR articles for free. You can download and use these articles on your blog. Most of these free PLR articles websites will request that you sign up to their newsletter. This is a small price to pay for getting free contents that you can use to set up your blog. You will receive permission to edit and use the downloaded contents on your blog/website. Below are two free PLR article sites you can use:

1. http://www.plrarticlepro.com
2. https://www.killerplrarticles.com/

The contents you will be provided from these two websites will be more than sufficient to fill your blog with high-quality contents that can make your blog look professional.

You have the option of writing at least ten articles on your own to fill your blog, but if you are looking to get started as quickly as possible, you can download articles from the above sites. Do not display any advertising on the blog; just make sure that what you have set up looks neat and organised.

Make sure you have a Privacy Policy and Contact Form on your blog. You can have this set up automatically by using the privacy policy plugin and contact form plugin that is available for WordPress. Go here to get them:

1. http://www.synclastic.com/plugins/privacy-policy/
2. http://wordpress.org/extend/plugins/contact-form-7/

With your blog fully set up, you will also need to prepare for a telephone call. In many cases, if you do not provide a real telephone number that you can be reached, you will not be approved by most CPA networks. The most popular CPA networks require telephone verification before approving applications into their network.

In most cases, an affiliate network expert from the CPA network will call to ask you a few basic questions about your modes of promotion. If you indicated that you will be doing web promotion for CPA offers, they will ask you to verify the site that you will be promoting their offers with, and whether you have any idea of the types of offers you would like to promote.

At this stage, you need to sound very confident and be sure of yourself regarding your promotional methods. Simply inform the affiliate network specialist that you will be developing websites that cater specifically to niches that are based on the type of CPA offers available within your network. The first site, which is your "dummy" site, should be the example of such a site.

If you have listed PPC as one of your options, you will likely be asked about your experience with PPC. Do not make it seem as if you are new to PPC. Just inform the specialist that you will be using Google AdWords, Yahoo PPC, and MSN AdCenter, to promote a range of offers. Do not drift into unnecessary details; just keep your answers simple and to the point. The CPA networks only want to know that a legitimate person is behind the application. Also, they are looking for their next "top affiliate" so they are basically "feeling you out" to see if you will be an asset to them. That is why you must have a professional website and appear that you have a plan on how best to promote the offers available within their network.

Some Top CPA Networks You Can Join

Now that you know the basics of getting accepted into CPA networks, the next thing to do is to apply to the various networks available. Your goal should be to get accepted into as many CPA networks as possible. The more networks you can get accepted into, the better for your business.

Below are some CPA Networks you can join:

1. http://www.azoogle.com
2. http://www.clickbooth.com
3. http://www.eadvertising.com
4. http://www.hydranetwork.com
5. http://www.incentaclick.com
6. http://www.marketleverage.com
7. http://www.maxbounty.com
8. http://www.neverblueads.com
9. http://www.offerweb.com

CHAPTER TWO

Choosing the Right CPA Offers

Let us assume that you have gone through and applied to the various CPA networks. The list is extensive and may change from time to time since some networks do go out of business or merge. The networks listed above are the ones that are the recommended ones that you can start with.

Now that you have been accepted into some networks, it is time to start selecting CPA offers that will bring in the money that you are looking for. Let us first go over the types of offers that you will find in a typical CPA Network.

EMAIL AND ZIP SUBMITS

This category is the easiest to convert but it is also the lowest-paying option available. You will need a huge volume to make considerable money using Zip and Email Submits. The typical "email submit" will pay you an average of $1.50 while the typical "zip submit" will pay you an average of $1.20. The payout rates will vary according to the CPA network.

The easiest offers to convert, from experience, are "zip

submit" offers. All the person must do is to submit their zip code in a form field, and you are paid. It is that simple, but you need to generate a lot of targeted traffic.

Zip submits convert at around 40% to 50%, so you should be looking to generate as much targeted traffic to these offers. When a person enters their zip code, you get paid, but there is a continuation to the form, so you want to make sure that the traffic that you are delivering to your zip submit offers is highly targeted.

Your leads must convert into a full lead sale for the advertiser. You are not paid extra when it does, but it keeps the advertisers happy, so quality is a must. Many people are making money with fake leads. This is not recommended as it will hurt your business in the long run.

Avoid the temptation of getting your friends and family members to start visiting your offers and entering their zip codes and email addresses. It can eventually lead to your account being terminated from the affiliate network or being banned from promoting any further zip submit offers. Deliver real traffic to the network and you will start making money from zip submit offers. The person only has to enter their zip code and you get paid, and they move on throughout the process of getting their free dinner for two. The person does not get a free dinner for two just by merely entering their zip code. You get paid for them doing that, but for the user to get their free dinner, they would need to complete a couple of free non-obligation offers. That is usually the "catch" with zip, and email submits offers.

Even though zip submit offers are good, you will not find as many when compared to email submit offers. These offers are available in abundance and usually pay a few cents more than zip submit offers. When a person submits their email address, you get paid, and as with the zip submit offer, they need to complete some free offers to be eligible to claim their prize.

Unlike zip submit offers, there is a bit more value in email submits because even if the person does not go on to continue the offer, at least their email address was captured. Along with agreeing to the privacy policy of the offer, the advertiser now has a new lead that they can market their products and services to.

That i's basically how email submits work. Your goal is to drive as much targeted traffic to the offer as possible. The conversion rate is a bit lower than the zip submits, so you can expect a conversion rate of approximately 30% to 35% on most email submit offers.

If your visitors are interested in gifts, then your rate could increase. When choosing an email to submit an offer, there are two things you can do to increase your conversion rate.

1. When possible, pre-sell the user on the offer if you are promoting the email submit offers on your website. You can write a paragraph of text that informs the user beforehand what they can expect from the offer. Let them know that by simply entering their email address, they may be eligible for some gifts. Whatever your email submit promotes, ensure you mention it in your pre-sell communication. You will find that your conversion rate increases when you pre-sell when compared to just pointing them to the offer.

2. Match your niche to a relevant email submit on offer. If your website is mainly about iPods, then you should find an IPOD email submit on offer to promote on your blog. Your conversion rate will skyrocket when you target your email submit offers specifically to your niche.

FINANCIAL OFFERS

Many CPA networks have a section of offers that cater exclusively to financial offers. These offers will range from credit scores, credit cards, loans, payday loans and debt relief. These are usually very high paying offers and can be high converting if you target them correctly. Bear in mind, however, that these offers do not require the person to buy anything. These are usually "lead" type offers, so you are paid for the person to submit their name, address, telephone number and other information into a form. Let us consider some of the offer types available.

1. Credit Score Offers

With these types of offers, the user has to sign up for a free credit report which includes credit monitoring. Since the credit monitoring is a free trial offer, the user must provide their credit card details since after the free trial the monitoring will be charged to the card on file. You will be paid from $15 to $20 for every person that signs up for the offer through your affiliate link.

To pre-sell credit score offers, you should write about the importance of checking your score, and if you have active monitoring, you can talk about how it has benefited you. What you are doing is that you are recommending the service beforehand to your visitors so that by the time they reach the offer, they will be willing to sign up. This will greatly increase your conversion rate on these kinds of offers.

2. Debt Relief Offers

These are great offers since you can genuinely pre-sell the user on the benefit of reducing debts. As the world economy is today, debt is a big problem, and most people are looking to reduce their debts as much as they can. On your blog, you can make a post about various ways of reducing debts and recommend the CPA offer. Of course, you subtly do this, as you do not want to come off as a car salesman pushing the person to complete the offer.

These offers range from $15 to $25 for every person you refer. If you have a blog that is geared towards debt relief, you should be able to get a few people each day to complete the offer. It is essential that whatever offer you decide to promote that your blog post or blog niche, in general, be specific to the offer. This will increase your conversion rate.

With debt relief, it is also good to share a personal story. It can be your story or the story of a friend. You just need to ensure that it is personable, engaging and that the result shows the importance of debt relief. That can also act as your pre-sell without having to push the user into the debt relief offer. It will be your goal to input the importance of debt relief into your visitor's head that will then lead them into completing your CPA offer.

When deciding on a debt relief offer, be sure you review all the offers available within the network. You want to choose one that pays high, but that the actual landing page has clear instructions regarding what the user needs to do to complete the offer. Select the landing page that you believe will result in the most conversions for you.

If after selecting an offer and it is not converting, switch to another one to see how that one performs. Test each offer for one week to get an idea of which one is performing the best, and then stick with the best performing offer. Do not settle for one offer without first testing a few others, as you could be losing out on some good money.

3. Payday Loan Offers

This is possibly one of the highest paying offers in the financial section. For example, NeverBlue.com has an offer paying as much as $42 for every payday loan application offer received. If you can generate enough targeted traffic to such CPA offers, you can make a substantial amount of money.

The best way to promote a payday loan offer is to relate such a loan to the user. Discuss the pros and cons of payday loans on your blog or website and provide tips about ensuring your users are approved for the loan, as well as tips to get repay it paid off as quickly as possible. By helping guide the user, you are building trust, and they will more than likely sign up with the payday loan that you recommend on your site.

It is about building trust with those offers. Most people looking for payday loans are in desperate need and actively looking for help. Your job is to provide insightful information along with recommending them a good payday loan company. You will be paid for every successful application.

If your blog or website is set up to specifically talk about payday loans or just about anything financial in general, you can stand to make a big profit from these offers. Keep your website targeted as much as possible to the CPA offers you are promoting, and you will see a good conversion rate with the offer.

As always, even though I mentioned NeverBlue.com, other networks offer payday loan offers as well. Review each network and choose the one that you believe will convert most. Test your offers and stick to the highest converting ones.

4. Weight Loss Offers

The weight loss market is huge. Everyone is looking to lose weight, shed fat, and look better. That means the opportunity to make good money with weight loss offers great. People are buying all kinds of offers hoping to reach their weight loss goals.

Many people might think that the weight loss market is highly saturated. There are offers out there, and there is a reason for that. It merely means that it is working. The average person does not buy just one offer or product. They typically buy multiple products hoping that at least one of them will work. As that is the case, promoting weight loss CPA offers can be extremely lucrative. Weight loss payment will range from $25 to $35, and usually, convert in the rage of 1% to 5%. The conversion rate has not been that great, but with enough traffic being generated to your offer, those $35 sales add up quickly.

One of the hottest products for weight loss is "Acai Berry" offers. By far the most popular product on the market due to all the hype and discussions made about it on television. Rachel Ray, Oprah Winfrey, and others have mentioned the benefits of "Acai Berry" on their TV shows. This has led to many "Acai Berry" products being developed.

Every major CPA network has an "Acai Berry" product available. The payout is in about $30 per sale. The best part of the "Acai Berry" offers is that most of them offer a "free trial" so the costs to the user are usually in the $4.95 – $5.95 range, which helps your conversion. The buyer of the product only has to pay shipping and handling costs to get their first bottle. With this being a major selling point, the conversion rate on these products is higher than traditional weight loss products.

5. Skincare and Anti-Aging Offers

This is a niche-specific category. It mostly targets women who have started seeing the effects of ageing on their skin. The major demographic is women 45 years and above. Many manufacturers claim that their products help to eliminate wrinkles and age spots.

Your goal is to find anti-ageing products that complement each other. That way, you can recommend both products on your blog and receive two sales instead of one. For example, you can find an offer that helps with eliminating wrinkles, and then find a follow-up product that helps with moisturizing or some other kind of benefits.

On your site, you will write about the real benefits for product number one, discuss how it has benefited you or someone you know (that is if you have tried the product). If you have not, then you can generalise the benefits based on what the manufacturer of the product has stated. If you can find reviews for the product as well, you can use those as part of your pre-sell pitch.

Then after mentioning product number one, you mention product number two as an addition to their overall skincare needs. By combining the two products, you are increasing your overall sales potential. Therefore, instead of making $30 on product number one, you can earn $60 in total sales. That is providing both offers are $30 per products.

What is good about the skincare market is that most of the offers also have a free trial. This means that in some cases, the buyer of the product only has to pay shipping and handling. Browse through all the CPA networks that you are a member of and find the skincare products that offer free trials as these will have higher conversion than those that people must pay in full. Once you find the two complementing products that offer a free trial, these will be the offers you promote on your website or blog.

6. Insurance Related Offers

People are always looking for good deals on insurance. Due to this, this market can also be a good money maker for CPA offers. It does not take much for a person to complete insurance-related CPA offers, especially the car insurance market. In most cases, all that is required is a name, address, email address and telephone number and you are paid for the lead.

The leads for insurance offers range from $9 up to $30; it all depends on how much information is needed on the form, and the type of insurance offer. In general, auto insurance leads pay much lower than health insurance leads. An average car insurance lead will pay you around $9, but a health insurance lead can pay you $30 per lead.

The reason for this is car insurance leads are easier to fill out, while health insurance leads are usually more in-depth and require more information. If you are looking for a bigger conversion, then you should stick with car insurance, as it is usually no obligation leads and does not require much from the user to submit.

You will also find that auto insurance leads are geared towards auto warranties. These offers target users who have expired warranties on their old cars but still require insurance coverage. Your website should discuss the importance of vehicle warranties and focus on old vehicles. Once you have discussed on your website the pros of getting a new vehicle warranty, then you can introduce them to the auto warranty offers that you are promoting.

Your conversion rate will be higher when you go about it this way than just setting up a random website and having auto warranty adverts on it. Ensure that every offer you promote is targeted.

CHAPTER THREE

Creating Sites Based on CPA Offers

The most lucrative ways of making money from CPA is to create niche-specific websites. Earlier, I talked briefly about creating blogs and targeting your blogs to your CPA offers, and I am going to focus on that in more details. My recommended content management system for creating these websites is WordPress. But before we move to setting up WordPress and building the website, we need to look at the inventory of the CPA companies. So, log into your CPA networks and go through their available offers.

What you should do is to look for offers that pay well, have very good affiliate banners and images that you can use on your website, and a good landing page. For example, let us say we decided we wanted to promote a weight loss offer. We review all the offers in the weight loss category, and we have decided to select an "Acai Berry" product. In some networks, you may have more than one "Acai Berry" product, so we will choose the one that offers a free trial with the best landing page and the highest payout.

After we have selected weight loss as our niche, and an

"Acai Berry" product, it is now time to dig deeper into what we will be talking about on the blog that we will be setting up. To find topics to write about, we need to do some keyword research. There are several tools you can use for your keyword research, but the two main tools are Google Keywords External Tool (https://adwords.google.com/select/KeywordToolExternal) and Free Word Tracker (http://freekeywords.wordtracker.com/).

By using these tools, you will come up with various keyword related topics that you can talk about on your blog or website. The purpose of the keyword research is to give your blog or website the chance to rank high in the search engines under a variety of long-tail keywords. In our "Acai Berry" example, we input the keyword "Acai Berry" into both the Google Keywords External Tool and the Free Word Tracker. We then evaluate the results.

Based on the results, we will take a few of the long-tail keywords, which are keywords that have a higher chance of achieving high rankings, along with more "buyer-oriented" keywords. A "buyer-oriented" keyword is typically associated with a product name. For instance, when we searched for "acai berry", among the results were "acai berry" products that were available for sale. These exact product names are what I refer to as "buyer-oriented". It means the searchers are looking for a particular product and more than likely if that product can be shown in a positive light, they will be inclined to buy.

An example of a non-buyer keyword would be something like "acai berry research". The people who search for the keyword might buy your product, but they could also be looking for more information about "Acai Berry" in general.

What you should target in your blog or website are the keywords that people are looking to take some sort of action.

If you want to take this a step further, you could narrow your keyword research by using the keyword "buy acai berry". This way, you are presented with the keywords people who want to buy the product are using. By putting the "buy" keyword in front of the product category, you are targeting the people who want to buy the product. Another trick is to replace the word "buy" with "purchase", and you will find another set of people who are ready to buy the product. You can also input the word "review", and you will find people who are looking for feedback, and these people can also turn into buyers.

Now that you have your keywords, the next step is to register a keyword-rich domain name that includes the keyword of your niche. The niche is "acai berry" in this case, so you should register a domain name with the keywords "acai berry" Once you have registered the domain name, you can now install WordPress and start writing and posting articles that cater to the keywords you have researched. If one of the keywords was "best acai berry to buy", that should be the title of your post, along with providing a short article about the topic. The "best acai berry to buy" that you are recommending is your CPA offer.

You will do this for all your "buyer keywords", and you will have a blog that concentrates on long-tail keywords specific to buyers who are interested in the CPA offer you are promoting. This is the best way to creating blogs or websites that are based on your CPA offers. This technique will work for every CPA product you will be promoting.

Your goal is to research CPA products, find buyer-keywords that relate to the products, register a keyword-rich domain name, and post articles on your blog that are based on your keywords.

If you follow this simple guide, you will create a network of blogs that promote a variety of CPA offers. This way, you will have a blog for every CPA offer you are promoting. You should do it this way, instead of stuffing all your CPA offers on one blog. Each blog should be tailored to your specific CPA offer.

CHAPTER FOUR

Writing Articles for CPA Profits

Another good way of making profits from CPA offers is by writing articles and submitting them to article directories. My focus with article writing has always been ezinearticles.com since they generate the most traffic out of all the directories. That is not to say that you cannot have success with other article directories.

We have already gone through the process of selecting CPA products, so I assume at this stage you will know what offers to promote. I am going to use our "Acai Berry" example again. Using the same keyword research that we have done previously, we would now have a set of keywords that we would want to target, and the articles we will be writing will be based on these keywords.

By default, you can only submit a maximum of 10 articles to EzineArticles.com when you register your first account. You should write ten high-quality articles that focus on your major keywords and submit them to EzineArticles.com. That should be your first step. Keep in mind that your resource box should be targeted to your

CPA product. For example, if your article discusses the "benefits of acai berry", then in your Resource Box, you will have the text "soft promoting" your CPA offer. I said "soft promoting" since you do not want it to sound like blatant advertising. Instead, make it appear more as a recommendation.

It is best to not direct link to the CPA offer, but instead, you can create a frame box for the offer that re-directs off your actual website. The person visiting your website or blog will still see your domain as the site they are browsing, but it is within a frame that is not visible, therefore masking the offer. Behind the scenes, your affiliate offer is loaded through a frame re-direct. This should be done for all your links within the article directories. You are allowed two links in your resource box. One can be for your "main blog" that utilizes the sites for CPA offers, and the second link will point to your CPA offer but using the masked page mentioned above.

With your ten articles written for EzineArticles.com, the next step is to write ten more articles, but this time these articles will be submitted to the other directories. You can mass submit these articles to as many directories as you want. Just ensure that the articles differ from the ones you submitted to ezinearticles.com. Repeat this process for every CPA offer niche that you have. By using this method, you are giving link juice to your niche CPA offer blogs, along with being able to achieve a few sales by direct linking to your CPA offer through a frame re-direct. It is a great way to utilize the power of article promotion.

Another important tip is to review the top articles and

authors within the niche you are promoting. For example, if your offer is "acai berry", your niche may be "weight loss" so you would want to review the top authors in that category along with the top articles in the category to know what they are doing to ensure you receive as many views as possible.

If you write your articles targeted to the specific buyer and long-tail keywords, there is a good chance your article can rank in the top ten under those particular keywords. To further increase the chances of your articles ranking high, you can take it a step further by social bookmarking each article you submit. The best way of going about social bookmarking is to use http://www.socialmarker.com. It is free of any charge.

CHAPTER FIVE

Creating Review Sites for CPA Profit

One of the most popular ways of making money with CPA is to create review-based sites. These sites act as a way of recommending a product. This is done by researching the various products you will be promoting and conducting keyword research to see how many people are searching for a review on the product.

For example, if you are promoting a product called "Acai Berry Blast", your site would be set up to write a review for that product along with other "Acai Berry" products. Your entire site is geared around writing reviews based on the main niche, which in this case is "Acai Berry".

That is basically what review sites are all about. Your goal should be to find at least two products within the niche to rate and review. Your CPA products should be ranked the best among the three products. The review needs to appear as natural as possible, so you do not over hype any of the products or belittle any of them. Try to sound as objective as possible while pointing out the pros and cons of the products.

Once you are done with your review, you will now have a site that provides what people are searching for, which is reviews on specific products. There are scripts you can use to set things up, but you can simply use WordPress to create the review sites.

You can also create a simple HTML template for the review site as well since the site will be based on these reviews and nothing more. Just remember that after reviewing all the products, you will then give a conclusion and list your recommended product(s) which will be your CPA offer.

CHAPTER SIX

Profiting from CPA Offers Using PPC

When you are setting up a PPC campaign for promoting CPA offers, it can be a hit or miss, depending on the campaign being promoted. That Is why it is going to be critical that you do some split tests when promoting your CPA offers, as some offers will convert while others may bomb.

1. **Good AdWords**

I like to test my offers with Google AdWords. It is fast and easy to set up, and you could start seeing conversions quickly if you have a winning campaign. The most crucial aspect of your PPC campaign will be how much you pay per click for your ad, and this will be based on your niche.

If we try our example before, which was "acai berry", then the competition in that niche for PPC is fierce. So, to get any exposure, you will need to place a high bid. The bid range for that keyword can range from $1 to $4 per click on average. Your bid amount can drop if you use the "buyer keywords" as mentioned earlier in this book.

Keywords with specific product names usually have a lower per-click rate than the "generic" ones. The searches may be less, but the per click rate will be lower and should have less competition generally. Your main competitors will be those trying to promote the same product.

For Google AdWords Pay Per Click, it will be best to use the Keyword External Tool. You will find keywords with a low Cost Per Click that are still receiving sufficient traffic to secure bids. Your goal is to get as many of these keywords as possible. When you combine these keywords, they can give you adequate traffic to generate a good income from your CPA offers. For instance, if you are promoting an email submit offer about free movie tickets, you should research the top movies coming out in the next few weeks or months and place bids on the keywords related to the movies. There are websites where you can review upcoming movies and place bids on those keywords and receive targeted traffic.

The Cost Per Click will be low and the conversion can be high and since your Cost Per Action offer is about getting free movie tickets and it is targeted to your niche.

When you create your ads for Pay Per Click with Google, it is best to have your ad units tightly woven together in terms of the keywords. Do not stuff your ad groups with keywords that are not relevant to each other.

For instance, you take your main ad group keyword, which in this case will be "buy acai" and within that ad group all the keywords will be about "buy acai". You can have keywords like "buy acai online" or "buy acai supplements". The ad group should have these types of ads within the group under the primary keyword term. You should also create a variety of ads within the ad group to match the keywords.

Once your ad groups are created and targeted, the landing page for each ad groups must be relevant. This means that for best results and to achieve a high-quality score from Google, your landing page should be set up to target the keywords within your ad group. The more targeted your landing page, the better your quality score will be for your Google Pay Per Click campaigns.

Remember that with your quality score, your cost per bid will drop in the long run, which should be the goal. Your intension should be to pay as little as possible for the traffic you are receiving, so you need to make the extra effort to keep your ad groups highly targeted along with your landing pages.

You will have to keep testing your advertising campaigns and eliminate the ad groups that are having low click-through rate or are not performing at all. If you keep ads with poor click-through rate, it can hurt your entire campaign, so you should continue to tweak your ads until you have reached an optimal CTR.

Always remember that with Pay Per Click, it is not a set-and-forget method until you have had a winning ad. To achieve takes testing. You will have some winners, and you will have some losers. The information provided here is mainly for Google, but it can work the same way for other ad networks.

2. Microsoft AdCenter

Microsoft Ad Center, though often overlooked, can provide you with a good return on your investment. Usually, the Cost Per Click is lower with Microsoft than with Google. The traffic is also a bit lower, so you will have to take the pros with the cons. You can find buyers with Microsoft, so you should give them a try with your CPA offers. The same principle applies to the grouping of your ads correctly, as this is wise to do for organising purposes. By grouping your advertising based on set keywords and landing pages, you can better target winning keywords from the losers.

Microsoft Pay Per Click keyword research should be done using their internal research tool. Do not make the mistake of using Google's tool as the numbers will be overstated. Use the data from Microsoft as it will give you a more accurate expectation of the amount of traffic you expect to receive. Before you embark on any campaigns, research the companies that are placing bids on the keyword that you are interested in, so you can analyse your competition correctly. Review what they are offering and how you can make your offer stand above theirs.

Remember that you do not have to go into a bidding war for the number one position to receive a good click-through rate. It is the title of your ad that is the most important. Asking a question and ensuring that the keyword being searched is in your ad title will increase your click-through rate and relevance.

You must give the internet user a reason to click on your ad and make sure that the reason is fulfilled on your landing page. If your offer is not in line with your ad title, your conversion rate will suffer. So, above all things, your title and your landing page must go pari passu. The title and the body or description of your ad lure the user to click, and your landing page should deliver exactly what your ad promised.

3. **Yahoo Search Network**

Yahoo Search Network is another great platform to use for your pay per click campaigns. The cost can range in the middle ground when compared to Microsoft AdCenter and Google AdWords.

As mentioned earlier, you should use Yahoo's suggestion tool for your pay per click campaigns. You will discover that the keywords that worked with the other two networks will do work here also. Most of your keyword research would have been done by the time you come to Yahoo Search Network, so it is a matter of seeing which offers appeal to Yahoo users.

As with Google AdWords, you should also use relevant landing pages. This is to guarantee that your keywords will be accepted when reviewed manually by Yahoo search editors. Some search editors deny users based on their landing pages not being relevant to the keywords they are bidding on. Therefore, always ensure that your landing pages are very relevant to your keywords.

Promoting Offers with Social Networks

Myspace and Facebook started as a means for people to keep in touch with their family and friends, and to meet new people. With billions of people being members of these two social networks, it has become some sort of a gold mine for internet marketers.

Both Facebook and Myspace have developed advertising platforms that allow users to market their offers to their audience. By opening their platforms to advertisements, people can directly target their offers to specific audiences.

With Myspace, you can get started with advertising easily. Just logon to https://advertise.myspace.com. The link takes you directly to Myspace's advertising programme. You can get started with as little as $25 and drive targeted clicks to your CPA offers. Before you rush to start your advertising campaign, first take note that the audience for Myspace is young people, so it may be hard to sell them products where they must spend money. Therefore, when going through your CPA offers, focus on offers that match the audience.

Since you can select the demographics for your ad campaigns, you can target the older folks on Myspace; that way, you can target those who are more willing and able to spend money. From experience, you should only market products where the audience has to spend money, like people over 30 years of age, especially if you are going to be promoting weight loss related offers.

A great tip for Myspace is that you should be original with your advertising campaigns. Your ad should be set up in such a way that it feels like you are talking directly to the people viewing your ad. Do not make your advertising sound like a pitch, like "Lose 20lbs in five days". Rather, you can say something like: "Are You Battling to Lose Weight?"

This title is more compelling; and in the body of the ad, you should highlight that you have been there as well and mention that you found a product that worked well for you. That type of ad can be very efficient on Myspace. The same thing goes for Facebook advertising.

The http://www.facebook.com/advertising/link is for Facebook's advertising. You can get started immediately, but there is a delay sometimes with their approval system. You have to wait for your advertising to be approved by the ad manager before you can proceed further with your advertising.

The best way to figure out what type of ads are being accepted on Facebook is to log into your Facebook account and review the ads being displayed. You may see a few CPA offers being promoted, and since Facebook is so large, you can directly compete for a piece of the cake by promoting that same offer.

Your ad must be very enticing since Facebook places a lot of relevance on CTR. If your ad has a good CTR, then they will show your ad more often. If they display your ads to thousands of people and they are not receiving good clicks, your ad could be buried. This means fewer impressions, which by default will result in little or no clicks.

Therefore, it will be crucial that the ad you create is very thought-provoking and enticing enough that the user will want to review what you have to offer. A lot of campaigns for reasonable offers die quickly due to having a poor title, so take the time to review the offers you see each day. If you see the same ad popping up often, it may mean that the title works, the offer is converting, and you can duplicate it.

Conclusion

We have come to the end of the book, but it should be looked upon as a new beginning for you, as you now have the necessary tools to get started with CPA offers. Do not overlook the tactics mentioned in this book. As simple as some of them are, they are very effective.

You may have to go through this book again to ensure that you have a clear outline of the types of offers you should target and the different ways you can go about targeting your campaigns.

Cost Per Action is here to stay, and people are already making a lot of money using the methods outlined in this book. The difference between those who are making money and those who are not is simple. It is people who take action that make the money.

Start joining Cost Per Action Networks, read the instructions about getting accepted into the networks. Once you are accepted, move forward with selecting campaigns and creating websites or blogs around those campaigns. It is when you take the initiative that you will start seeing results.

I wish you all the best!